Original title:
Star-Crossed Sonnets

Copyright © 2025 Creative Arts Management OÜ
All rights reserved.

Author: Elliot Harrison
ISBN HARDBACK: 978-1-80567-860-1
ISBN PAPERBACK: 978-1-80567-981-3

Beneath the Same Stars

Two lovers gaze at the night sky,
But one says, "Look, a pizza pie!"
"It's not a pie, it's a bright star!"
"Would be great with cheese from afar."

Their hearts entwined like tangled lights,
They argue on these starry nights.
Her dreams of romance fill the air,
His dreams of food? Beyond compare.

Celestial Wounds

He fell for her like an asteroid,
But love's a road that's often annoyed.
"Do you like my comet-like hair?"
"Please land it here, it's giving me scare."

While dodging meteors in their way,
They trip, they laugh, they dance and sway.
Through cosmic chaos, they still find,
A love that's quirky, one of a kind.

Echoes of Promise

In the silence of the vast expanse,
Their whispers echo in a silly dance.
"Did you just hear that alien call?"
"It's just my tummy... I'm hungry, y'all!"

They promise stars beneath the moon,
While plotting meals that come too soon.
And though their journeys may go far,
They'll return home for a candy bar.

Cosmic Journeys

On spaceships made of cardboard boxes,
They travel through the universe's oxes.
"Is that a nebula or my old sock?"
"Let's call it colors; it really rocks!"

They laugh through light-years, time and space,
Exploring every goofy place.
With silly maps and snacks in tow,
They navigate where funny winds blow.

Starlit Serendipity

In a cosmic dance, we twirl and spin,
Fumbling clumsily, with goofy grins.
A comet's tail, a sparkly surprise,
We trip and laugh 'neath the wink of the skies.

Bumping into planets, we share a toast,
To all the chaos we love the most.
Galaxies giggle as we spin around,
In this whimsical world where joy is found.

Celestial Conflicts

Oh, Mercury's speeding, can't keep up the race,
While Jupiter's laughing, oh what a face!
It's a lunar brawl, with asteroids at play,
We dodge the debris, in a comical way.

Venus throws tantrums, all sultry and sweet,
While Mars is just sulking, oh can't take the heat.
Constellations argue, a tapestry spun,
Yet in all this madness, we still find our fun.

Magnetic Hearts

Your pull is too strong, like gravity's kiss,
Yet I can't help but trip, what a cosmic twist!
In a supernova of laughter, we collide,
Our quirks and our charms are a bumpy ride.

With magnets, we're tangled, what a silly sight,
Two celestial fools, in love's funny light.
We orbit around, like moons without haste,
Finding joy in the chaos, no moment to waste.

Fragments of Infinity

In a galaxy far, with giggles so loud,
We break into stardust, a shimmering crowd.
With every mishap, a spark we ignite,
Who knew clumsiness could feel so right?

From asteroids barking, to comets that dance,
Our journey's a jest, a whimsical chance.
Through fragments of infinity, we roam with delight,
In this hilarious waltz, we shine through the night.

Diverging Paths of Light and Dark

Two lovers stand, both dressed in black,
One shouts, "I'm off!"
The other, with a snack,
Replies, "I'll eat this tot!

They meet at dusk, where shadows grow,
One says, "Look, a star!"
The other trips on toe,
They giggle near and far.

With every twist, a silly dance,
One leaps, the other trips,
They chuckle at their chance,
And share popcorn from their lips.

A meteor whizzes, they duck for cover,
Then laugh, 'That was close!'

Whispers of the Universe's Embrace

A cosmic joke, they trade in jest,
She claims to see a sphere,
He insists it's just the best,
Of space pizza right here!

They bicker on the meaning of stars,
"I say they're just lights!"
"You mean out of cars?"
"That's entirely wrong fights!"

With every wish upon a flare,
"I'll wish for more fries!"
She gasps, "How unfair!"
As they laugh beneath the skies.

In their galaxy, giggles collide,
A cosmic broomstick race,
Through starlit hugs they glide,
In laughter's warm embrace.

Infinite Yearning in Cosmic Silence

In spaces vast, a comet flies,
She yells, "Catch that!"
He simply rolls his eyes,
"It's just a glowing brat!"

They craft their dreams on cosmic chalk,
With giggles, they draw,
An alien wearing a frock,
"Is he even in law?"

Oh, the nights of pondering fate,
"Do black holes eat bread?"
"Only if it's great!"
"Well, that explains Fred!"

Beneath the laughter, stardust swirls,
As they share their fears,
In the quiet cosmic whirls,
They toast with fizzy cheers.

Tides of Fate in the Ether

Two nerds with telescopes collide,
He says, "Look at that wisp!"
She roars with laughter inside,
"That's just my desperate grip!"

They chart the moon and make a bet,
"I'll jump if it gnaws!"
"While I'll just forget,
A whale in a tux with claws!"

The tides shift with each cosmic joke,
As planets begin to twirl,
His side barely holding smoke,
Her laughter's a silver swirl.

In the ether, they splash about,
With wide, starry grins,
Building dreams, they hop and shout,
In empty cosmic bins.

Fated Encounters in Twilight

In a café, I spilled my drink,
Across from you, I couldn't think.
You laughed so hard, it made a scene,
I just blushed, my face turned green.

Your dog stole fries right off my plate,
And here we are, it feels like fate.
You wink and say, 'I'll get you some,'
And just like that, my heart goes thrum.

We walked outside, you tripped and fell,
I caught your hand, or so you tell.
A clumsy dance beneath the stars,
You dropped my heart, but got your cars.

Now every date's a little wild,
Who knew that fate could be so styled?
Your laughter rings, we're quite the pair,
Just clumsy souls caught unaware.

Celestial Whispers Beneath the Moon

We met while stargazing on a hill,
You said, 'I'm pretty sure I'm ill!'
Your telescope was broken too,
But still you swore you saw a clue.

You pointed up, I saw your smile,
The moon looked down, it stayed a while.
You claimed your heart was made of cheese,
It felt so right, if you'd just sneeze!

You tossed a pebble, called it Mars,
I laughed so hard, it jarred the stars.
We mapped the skies with silly names,
And danced ourselves into love games.

Our cosmic chat was quite a spree,
Your laughter floated, wild and free.
We'll chart the night, with puns anew,
A celestial play just me and you.

Love's Distant Horizon

Chasing dreams on a boardwalk late,
Found you munching popcorn; what a fate!
You dropped a kernel into my drink,
I laughed so hard, thought I might sink.

Your hat flew off, it danced in air,
You chased it down without a care.
It landed right on top of my head,
We both just laughed, and then you said:

'Is this a sign of love divine?'
I shrugged and sipped your drink of wine.
We watched the sunset; quite a scene,
Together, we made the clumsiest team.

With sandy feet and salty skin,
You made me laugh with every grin.
Like ships we sailed, our hearts in tow,
Our love, a quirky, fun-filled show.

Chasing Shadows of the Heart

Underneath the flickering lights,
We danced through alleyways of sights.
I stepped on toes, you faked a fall,
Together we managed quite the brawl.

A shadow jumped, you screamed so loud,
At first, I thought you'd lost your crowd.
We laughed so hard, like giggling foes,
As we chased shadows, and silly prose.

Your phone went off; a ringtone blast,
It was your mom, she called you fast.
You answered, then went on a rant,
I lost it all; a laughing chant.

Our hearts beat out a funky song,
In this crazy dance, we can't go wrong.
With jokes and jibes, we chase the dark,
Two silly souls igniting a spark.

Love's Celestial Voyage

Two comets raced across the sky,
With cheesy grins, they flew so high.
They tripped on stardust, oops, what a mess,
But laughed and danced in cosmic dress.

A meteor shower crashed their date,
They dodged and weaved, oh what a fate!
With ice cream moons and rocket pies,
They found love 'neath clumsy skies.

The Pulse of the Milky Way

In the heart of galactic fun,
Two planets spun 'round, what a run!
They skipped through rings of cosmic cheer,
With whispers sweet that only they could hear.

Galactic gossip flew like stars,
They giggled 'bout Jupiter's odd cars.
While Neptune danced in spiky shoes,
They twirled 'round black holes, avoiding the blues.

Forbidden Galaxies

She was from Venus, he hailed from Mars,
They laughed so hard beneath blinking stars.
With cosmic law declaring them foes,
They threw space parties, shushed all their woes.

Galaxies giggled at their sneaky dance,
A comet swooped by, giving romance a chance.
In this quirky universe full of quirks,
They found love's spark, despite the quirks.

A Universe Apart

They penned sweet notes on asteroids bright,
Each word a flicker, a cosmic light.
Though lightyears separated their beams,
In every odd twinkle, they chased their dreams.

With rocket-powered love, they'd tease the dark,
Posting their feelings like a shooting spark.
Though planets rolled their eyes on the sides,
Their silly love was a galaxy ride.

Fractured Light

In the sky where dreams collide,
A neon cat on a cosmic ride.
It winks and laughs at grand designs,
With grilled cheese floating in starry lines.

Galaxies spin like a dizzy dancer,
While planets compete in a romantic prancer.
Asteroids whisper jokes so bold,
While comets play tag with tales retold.

Black holes laugh, consuming the fun,
Swallowing hopes like a chocolate bun.
And stardust sprinkles on everyone's head,
While aliens join in, dancing instead.

Yet here we are, on this blue ball,
Caught in a tangle, we trip and fall.
But amidst the laughter, we'll find our way,
In this cosmic joke, let's dance and sway.

Whispers of the Cosmos

If planets had secrets, they'd giggle and gleam,
Swapping tales over cosmic ice cream.
Mars claims he's the best at hide and seek,
While Venus just blushes and takes a peek.

Jupiter spins with a wink and a grin,
While Saturn's rings boast of where to begin.
But Mercury zips around, so fast and spry,
Chasing the tale that's up in the sky.

The sun tells knock-knock jokes to the stars,
While moons play tag with comets from Mars.
The Milky Way giggles with every light,
Spreading laughter with each twinkling sight.

In this cosmic circus, we twirl about,
With jesters and dreams, never a doubt.
So let's join the laughter, let's take flight,
With whispers of the cosmos, everything's bright!

Tangled in Time

Time's a jester with tricks up its sleeve,
Winking at moments we can't believe.
It skips and hops, a silly ol' fool,
Making us dance to its whimsical rule.

Yesterday's socks are lost in the fray,
While tomorrow's plans are just on delay.
The present's a trickster, a slippery chap,
Leading us round in a colorful map.

Old clocks are chuckling as floors start to squeak,
Time travel's a party, but oh, it's unique!
We fumble and stumble on paths that we roam,
In this tangled web of an endless home.

But laughter remains, our sweet escape,
In moments of chaos, we happily shape.
For tangled we are, through ages and rhyme,
Just playful souls in this game called time.

The Enchanted Sky

Look up above, what a sight to see,
A cloud shaped like a dancing bee.
The stars are convinced they're the new rock stars,
Singing their songs from Venus to Mars.

A moonbeam slips on a silvery shoe,
As the auroras plot their next dance too.
They twirl and swirl in colors so bright,
Creating a rave in the depths of the night.

The constellations gossip, they giggle and tease,
What's stronger, a comet or a gentle breeze?
And while Earth spins, we laugh and we cheer,
In this enchanting sky, there's nothing to fear.

So let's twinkle and shine, join the cosmic glee,
As we float in the laughter of the galaxy.
With each twinkling star, we share a good laugh,
In the enchanted sky, we'll dance on the path.

Moonlit Encounters

In the night, we trip and fall,
On romantic dreams, we brawl.
You spilled your drink, I touched my nose,
Our dance began, a clumsy prose.

The moon above, it starts to giggle,
As we two wobble and wiggle.
Your shoe just flew, oh what a sight,
We laugh until the morning light.

With matching socks, we've made a scene,
A love so strange, surreal, and keen.
We chase the fireflies in a haze,
And bump into trees, in playful craze.

Yet here we stand, with hearts so bold,
Chasing jesters, while hugs unfold.
With every quirk, our spirits blend,
This moonlit dance, it will not end.

Lovers in the Twilight

In twilight's glow, we start to fumble,
With silly jokes, we laugh and stumble.
You made a face, I couldn't breathe,
A comedy show, oh what a reprieve!

We tried to kiss, but missed the mark,
Landed on noses—what a spark!
Your wiggle dance is such a sight,
As fireflies join our tangled flight.

We painted walls with candy dreams,
And splattered paint, or so it seems.
Two clumsy hearts in sync tonight,
With giggles bright against the night.

So here we are, in giggly glee,
With every misstep, you're still with me.
In twilight's charm, our love's grown wild,
A joyful mess, both free and styled.

Cosmic Collisions

In cosmic dance, we trip through stars,
Dodging planets, bumping cars.
You swirled about, an awkward sight,
As meteors fell with gleeful might.

Your spaceship's name was "Fuzzy Love,"
A charming ride, no stars above.
We laughed so loud, the comets swayed,
A dance-off here, our jokes displayed.

We crashed right into a moonlit bar,
And offered drinks to each bizarre star.
With quirky chats, we spin and twirl,
In this circus, you're my pearl.

Through cosmic realms, our laughter flew,
In every crash, I found you true.
Two celestial fools, a perfect find,
In chaotic space, our hearts entwined.

Destiny's Dance

The fates had plans, or so they thought,
But all they brewed was a silly plot.
With two left feet, we take our stance,
Awkwardly caught in destiny's dance.

You twirled and stumbled, what a sight,
As we two spun in sheer delight.
A duck-like waddle, we own this floor,
With laughter echoing, we beg for more.

Each misstep brings a bright surprise,
With glitter falling from the skies.
Our partners are quirks that make us whole,
In this grand jive of a dancing soul.

So take my hand, let's whirl away,
No grace, no rhythm, just here to play.
With smiles as bright as stars in trance,
We make our mark in destiny's dance.

Astral Dreams

In a galaxy far, quite absurd,
Two comets collided, such a strange word.
They laughed as they tripped on stardust trails,
Wishing on wishes that danced like whales.

Planets swapped tales of pizza and cheese,
While meteors rushed by with a gentle tease.
Love in the cosmos, a wobbly sight,
With UFOs giggling at the cosmic light.

Aliens dreamt of a crazy romance,
Creating a dance in a zero-grav prance.
They joked with the moons, all round and full,
That love's just a game of push and pull.

So if you find love in a weird place,
Just laugh with the stars, keep up the pace.
In this cosmic circus, fun never ends,
With laughter entwined, let the universe bend.

Cosmic Threads

In the fabric of space, where giggles abound,
Lovers stitch stories with laughter, unbound.
Nebulas dance in a quilt of delight,
While quirky fairies sprinkle hearts in the night.

A quasar chuckled at a black hole's plight,
As gravity pulled love with all of its might.
Jupiter winked, it's a giant of fun,
In the great cosmic play, we all are one.

Venus and Mars had a playful debate,
About which of them holds the best date.
Comets zipped by with a whoosh and a cheer,
While aliens threw confetti, spreading good cheer.

So gather your stardust, let laughter ignite,
In this universe bright, love feels just right.
With each cosmic stitch, a tale to be spun,
In the tapestry woven, we're all just a pun.

Love's Entropy

In a chaotic dance of swirling delight,
Two atoms collided in the heat of the night.
They giggled as bonds formed a delightful mess,
In a universe wild, less is more than stress.

Entropy sparked in their playful embrace,
With each little quirk, a hilarious race.
Electrons were dancing in circles so wide,
While protons exchanged playful pokes side by side.

They tossed out the rules, with a wink and a grin,
Knowing that love sometimes feels like a spin.
With laughter they found in the cosmic ballet,
It's the silly mistakes that brighten the day.

So fumble and tumble, let chaos unfurl,
In the swirling dance of this quirky old world.
Love's like a formula that's hard to define,
But with humor and chaos, it surely will shine.

Gravity of the Heart

With a plop and a thud, love fell from the skies,
Like a meteor shower of crumbs and goodbyes.
It spun and it whirled, like a wacky old game,
Making us giggle as hearts dropped their claim.

The gravity pulled, like an awkward old joke,
While planets all chuckled and sometimes provoked.
In this tangled dance, emotions took lead,
As love's blooper reel filled the hearts with a breed.

Asteroids bounced, playing tag in the dark,
While satellites snickered, igniting a spark.
It's space's odd humor, a cosmic report,
Where laughter's the fuel for an amiable court.

So if you find love that plays with your heart,
Embrace all the giggles; don't worry, take part.
For in this wild cosmos, we giggle and play,
And the gravity of love will always stay.

The Lament of Lost Time

On Tuesday it was sunny blue,
But then the rain just followed through.
I lost my hat up in a tree,
And there it sways, just mocking me.

My clock strikes twelve at half-past eight,
I think my plans are just too late.
I dropped my sandwich, what a waste,
Now I must lunch on soggy paste.

I meant to nap beneath the sun,
But now I'm sleeping, outdone by fun.
The day has vanished, blink, it's gone,
And yet my worries carry on.

So here I ponder with a sigh,
As each minute seems to fly.
With Luna's laugh, it feels quite fine,
For lost time's just a laugh divine.

Astral Serenade

Out in space, they dance and spin,
A cosmic jig with flaps and grins.
Galaxies twirl on the sideline,
While comets groove like it's all fine.

Mars tried to sing a rom-com song,
But missed a beat, it felt all wrong.
Jupiter laughed and joined the beat,
A waltzing planet, can't be beat.

The stars giggled, shooting by,
"Why so serious?" the Milky Way sighs.
Orion cracks a dazzling joke,
While Saturn wears a bright bow cloak.

And in this void, we twirl and sway,
Swaying 'neath the beams of play.
The universe, a dance routine,
A funny cosmic, lively scene.

Fragments in Orbit

My spaceship's stuck with bubble gum,
The kind that's chewy, what a scrum!
Each orbit takes a breath away,
A journey lost, oh what a play!

Asteroids with faces grinning wide,
They rock and roll, they laugh and glide.
My fuel is popcorn, cheers abound,
While space squirrels scamper all around.

I tried to catch a falling star,
But missed it clearly, too bizarre!
It teased me with its glittered light,
Then zipped away, oh what a fright!

With stardust stuck upon my shoe,
I float and flaunt, it feels brand new.
Fragments twirl, a stellar spree,
In orbit's dance, I'm wild and free.

Intergalactic Yearning

In a galaxy, far, far away,
I crave some coffee, hip-hip-hooray!
A barista robot brews and steams,
But spills it all, oh, shattered dreams.

I wish for bagels, warm and toasted,
But they are made of stardust, roasted.
Each bite's a crunch, and then it flies,
As moonbeams light up hungry eyes.

Romancing aliens, with three green eyes,
They flirt with quips and cosmic sighs.
I offer snacks made of pure charm,
And in this jest, they find the balm.

So here I float, with laughter bold,
In space's arms, I find my gold.
Galactic love, a quirky tune,
With snacks and laughs, we dance till noon.

Bridging Galaxies

In a universe wide, our hearts collide,
Like two clumsy comets, on a wild ride.
Your laugh echoes 'round, it's quite a delight,
But sometimes you trip when I hold you tight.

Building bridges of giggles, we float in the air,
Dodging awkward moments, without a care.
I drop the sweet snacks, they're all on the floor,
But your smile's so bright, I just want more.

Space hiccups might send us to separate zones,
But our goofy love will ignite cosmic tones.
With fumbles and laughter, we paint the night sky,
In our silly galaxy, we'll forever fly.

The Universe's Plea

Oh universe, can you hear my call?
I'm ready to trip on your cosmic sprawl.
With planets a-spinning and stars in a fuss,
Can't you guide my heart straight to hers, without a bus?

I promise to share my last piece of pie,
While gazing at moons that dip low and high.
But if I slip on a cosmic banana,
Will you save me from love's hilarity drama?

As galaxies wobble, we'll dance on a whim,
Resolving odd quarrels on love's silly hymn.
The universe chuckles, a joyride of fate,
Letting us trip while we learn how to skate.

Longing Across Time

Through echoes of ages, our hearts intertwine,
But timing is tricky, like a flat tire's whine.
You send me texts that are perfect and bright,
Yet I keep replying at the oddest of nights.

Oh, time traveler, can you see what I mean?
When I trip on my words like a scene from a dream?
You're all in my thoughts, but miles away,
Just like socks lost in the drier's dismay.

With the past and the future, we dance and we play,
But our dates seem to float like a leaf on a bay.
So here's to the moments, the giggles and sighs,
In a time-warping love, with your joy in my eyes.

Love's Orbit

In a wobbly orbit, we circle with grace,
You're moonwalking, I'm tripping—what a clumsy embrace!
While other loves fizzle, we burst into flames,
You roast me with puns, and I laugh at your names.

Every quirk that you own spins my heart in its groove,
With jokes that bounce light years, we constantly move.
Like meteors blazing through skies full of cheers,
We'll conquer this cosmos, dismiss all the fears.

Your laughter's the music, your smile's the sun,
In this orbit of love, we both always run.
Though planets might watch, and stars take a blink,
In our own little world, it's silly, don't you think?

Love Beyond Horizons

In a cosmos vast, two hearts collide,
Like comets that twirl, in a cosmic ride.
They glance with glee, forget the rules,
While gravity pulls, and they act like fools.

One says, "Let's dance on Saturn's rings!"
The other retorts, "I'll take wine and flings!"
With laughter that echoes through moonlit skies,
They trip on stardust, exchanging sly eyes.

Galaxies giggle at their silly plight,
As they argue over whose turn to hold tight.
In a rocket fueled by love and snacks,
They fly through the skies while dodging asteroids' hacks.

But in the end, it's a playful fate,
For laughter is sweet when love is innate.
Together they shine, like suns in a blip,
Forever entwined on their cosmic trip.

Celestial Heartstrings

Two hearts in orbit, tangled in jest,
They play hide and seek in a universe blessed.
With twinkling eyes, they dance through the night,
Tripping on stardust, it feels so right.

"You take my heart!" the one quips and beams,
"But I've misplaced it among cosmic dreams!"
They laugh over galaxies, and it's clear to see,
Love is a joke, written in destiny.

With supernova pops and asteroid dives,
They ride on the waves of romantic lives.
While aliens cheer, sipping space bubbly,
These lovers create chaos, all sweet and cuddly.

But as comets pass, they start to pout,
"Who packed the snacks? I'm starting to doubt!"
Yet with every mishap that triggers a grin,
They know in this madness, true love will win.

Clash of Celestial Lovers

In the realm of the stars, where lovers can spar,
Two heroes collide on a quirky bazaar.
"You stole my stardust!" one angrily cries,
"Only because it lit up your big, silly eyes!"

They bicker and banter, a cosmic debate,
Trading playful insults that seal their fate.
With a flick of a wrist, one launches a flare,
The other just chuckles and throws back some air.

Through black holes they tumble, spinning in space,
Laughing at gravity's futile embrace.
On Mars, they argue; on Venus, they kiss,
Disguised cosmic chaos, absurdly bliss.

With laughter as fuel for their intergalactic run,
They glow like supernovas, a pair always fun.
In a universe swirling with mischief and cheer,
These lovers create magic wherever they steer.

Cosmic Melancholy

In the quiet of space, where stars softly sigh,
Two souls are adrift, with a twinkle goodbye.
They miss each other more than the moon,
Each search so futile, yet they hum a tune.

"I swear we were galaxies—lost in a dance!"
"But we tripped through the cosmos without a chance!"
Memories linger like dust on their hearts,
In the comedy of fate, it's just how love starts.

Yet laughter emerges when stars start to mope,
For in every dark alley, there's always a hope.
"We might be lost, but I'll bring the snacks!"
Their spirits reclaim joy, as laughter attacks.

With each cosmic tear, they shine even bright,
For melancholy's a phase in their endless flight.
Together they navigate the cosmic plight,
Finding humor in love, as they roam the night.

Glimmering Love in a Shadowed Realm

In the dark I found a shoe,
A sign of romance askew.
We twirled beneath the cosmic plight,
Our giggles echoed through the night.

Frogs sang tunes of love's sweet jest,
While mismatched socks put hearts to the test.
With every leap, we danced around,
Lost in laughter, our love unbound.

Chasing shadows like kids at play,
Missing the mark, yet bold in the fray.
With clumsy steps, we took the plunge,
Two hearts entangled in a jolly lunge.

In this realm where giggles gleam,
We're scattered stars in a silvery dream.
Though tangled up in our droll fate,
Together we shimmer and can't be late.

Dualities of the Cosmic Dance

In the cosmos, a clumsy whirl,
We tripped over space, oh what a twirl!
Your foot in my soup, my hair in a knot,
Yet who would've guessed, we loved quite a lot.

With moons and planets aligning askew,
We laughed through the stars—a cosmic brew.
Your polka dots clashed with my stripes,
Together we spun, avoiding the gripes.

Coffee cups tilted, a comet's tail,
Each sip we took told a wacky tale.
The universe chuckled at our silly spree,
Two oddball heroes in a grand symphony.

As we danced through the nebula's glow,
Our love story's written in dazzling show.
With winks and nods from the heavens above,
We're proof that the universe laughs with love.

The Velvet Silence of Unraveled Promises

Whispers in velvet, oh what a tease,
Unraveled promises swirling with ease.
You said 'forever', I said 'forever', too,
But then tripped over my own shoe.

In the silence, giggles explode,
As tangled dreams start to erode.
You wore a grin like a mischievous cat,
Promising stars while I chased a rat.

Our vows floated like balloons on a string,
A wild ride in the chaos we bring.
Each laugh echoed through silly mishaps,
We were destined to chart the oddest maps.

In this quiet chaos, love wears a crown,
A patchwork quilt of ups and down.
With every promise we've tangled and spun,
Laughter remains—our truest fun.

Petals Falling Through Starlit Vows

Petals drift down on a breezy night,
We danced in circles, oh what a sight.
Your shoelaces tied up my will to flee,
Yet here we are, as sweet as can be.

In the starlit vows, we found our place,
Tripping on laughter, we set the pace.
You spilled the punch—what a marvel, indeed!
Our love's a garden, despite all the weeds.

With each crooked smile and wink on the way,
We crafted our tales in a whimsical play.
Falling petals, a merry parade,
In this silly dance, no hearts will fade.

As we bask in our clumsy delight,
Together we shine, our futures so bright.
In this floral chaos, we laugh and we vow,
To cherish each moment, here and now.

Ephemeral Dreams

In dreams we're daft, it seems to be,
We dance on clouds like fries in grease.
With laughter loud, we spin with glee,
Yet wake to find our dreams in fleece.

A pizza slice than moons more bright,
We chase them on this wobbly bike.
Each twinkle makes our hearts take flight,
But gravity? Oh, what a hike!

Those dreams slip by like fish in streams,
We think they'd stay, they play and tease.
Yet "ephemeral"—I should have guessed,
Just like my lunch, poof! Gone with ease.

So here's to dreams that love to play,
They leave us laughing, night and day.
We'll catch them all, come what may,
And snack on hope like it's gourmet!

Radiance of Regret

My heart's a light bulb, flickering bright,
  You see my grin, but not the plight.
  Regrets like stars in endless skies,
Each twinkle winks—oh, how time flies.

  I dropped my chance, it rolled away,
  I should have said what I would say.
  A comical twist, a misplaced jape,
    Turns love into a wobbly shape.

  With every cringe and silly jest,
    I rue the day I tried my best.
  Yet here I stand, with humor's zest,
  Joking flaws while I jest and quest.

  So let me laugh, despite the pain,
  I'll wear my missteps like a chain.
  For radiance flickers, joy is gain,
  In every blunder, there's a refrain!

Fated Pathways

Two fools collide on paths unknown,
With shoes untied and seeds hewn stone.
Our hearts like popcorn, pop and sway,
We trip and tumble, come what may.

With signs that point to nowhere fast,
We follow instincts that never last.
A compass spun by giggles bright,
Leads us in circles, day and night.

When fate once called, we missed the line,
But laughter's currency feels divine.
With fated blunders, we shine and chime,
Our love's the punchline, every time.

So here we are, on twisted lanes,
With silly grins and love's refrains.
Let's dance through life, despite the gains,
In all our mishaps, joy remains!

The Nebula of Us

In cosmic kitchens, we both cook,
With recipes (mostly) off the hook.
A dash of chaos, a pinch of grace,
We stir confusion in this space.

Like comets tangled in a chase,
Our love's a whirlwind, fast-paced race.
With stardust sprinkles on our cake,
Every bite's laughter—make no mistake.

Galaxies of giggles eagerly grow,
As mishaps orchestrate our show.
From burnt toast stars to moonlit sighs,
We float through life with gleeful eyes.

The nebula swirls, it's quite the mess,
Yet here we are, feeling blessed.
With love that's funny, what a zest,
In this wild chaos, we find rest!

Nebulas of Forgotten Promises

In the depths of space, love took a nap,
Promises made, but fell with a flap.
Asteroids chuckled at our silly plight,
As comets zoomed past, giving us fright.

Galaxies spun while we simply twirled,
Dancing on stardust, our timing unfurled.
Forgotten vows drifted like old socks,
Floating in orbits, lost in paradox.

Nebulas sighed, rolling their bright eyes,
Witnessing us reach for improbable skies.
With each twinkle, fate played its hand,
While we stood laughing, all things unplanned.

The Cosmos Cries Out for Us

Oh heavens above, what a cosmic show,
How did we end up on this merry-go?
Space hiccups echoed our love's silly dance,
While planets engaged us in a clumsy romance.

Nebulae swirled, doing the moonwalk,
Engaging us lightly in some starry talk.
A supernova winked as we faltered too,
"Oh come, let's all watch this drama ensue!"

The Milky Way laughed, sharing our woes,
Each stumble and fumble, the laughter it grows.
In stellar forums, they'll write our tale,
Two fools in the void, destined to fail.

Starlit Passages of Passion

In the warm glow of flickering light,
We stumbled through paths that felt just right.
Each step a misstep, like dance in the air,
Waving to meteors, unaware they stare.

Galactic blunders colored our days,
With satellites giggling at our clumsy ways.
We twirled through constellations, our feet all a mess,
While Venus just chuckled, "You two need less stress!"

In starlit halls where laughter abounds,
Our silly mistakes became joyful sounds.
With meteor showers granting wishes galore,
We fumbled for love, still wanting much more.

Bound by Celestial Forces

Two hearts colliding in a spiral embrace,
Drawn together by fate's goofy grace.
Gravity giggled, pulling us tight,
While Saturn just shook its rings with delight.

With each solar flare, we stumbled and spun,
Like planets in orbit, we weren't quite done.
Astrological jokes in the time warp we make,
As quasars blink twice, for heaven's sake!

Bound by the forces we can't override,
With each galactic hiccup, we took it in stride.
Through the cosmic chaos, joy was the guide,
In a universe laughing, we shimmered with pride.

Cosmic Ballet of Lost Souls

In a dance of fate, we twirl and sway,
Tripping on dreams, we stumble and play.
Galactic mischief fills the night air,
With comets teasing in a cosmic affair.

A meteor winks, then falls with a boom,
As we giggle in the dark, sharing our gloom.
Planets collide, but we laugh at the mess,
Spinning in chaos, we call it success.

Aliens peek from their starry retreats,
Confused by our flailing and comical beats.
The universe chuckles, it knows we are wild,
Two cosmic jesters, forever a child.

So let's dance on this stage, where we bumble and weave,

Under the watchful eyes of stars that believe.
In this ballet of folly, we joyfully glide,
For lost souls find solace when laughter's our guide.

Astral Dreams Beyond Time

In dreams we soar on stardust wings,
Juggling moons while the universe sings.
Tickling black holes with playful delight,
As time rolls around like a runaway kite.

Nebulas giggle, a colorful show,
While we dance to rhythms only we know.
Asteroids clank in a raucous refrain,
As galaxies twirl, oh, what a strange chain!

We paint the cosmos with laughter and cheer,
Echoing joy through the vastness, oh dear!
With a wink to the comets that dash to and fro,
We whisper our dreams, hoping they'll grow.

Through time and space, we weave the absurd,
While celestial bodies just chuckle unheard.
In this realm of the quirky, we chatter and scheme,
Creating a tapestry stitched with our dream.

Constellations of Longing

In the sky hang our wishes, like stars in a map,
Tangled tales of love, with a wink and a clap.
Hoping the cosmos will answer our call,
While the moon grins slyly and takes in it all.

We count the constellations, a cosmic charade,
Falling for dreams, we're silly yet unafraid.
The Big Dipper dips in a puddle of light,
As we chase our desires through the quirky night.

With each shooting star, we giggle and squeak,
Mumbling sweet nonsense, oh, how we sneak.
Galactic giggles ride the starfished breeze,
As we grasp at the heavens with whimsical ease.

In this cosmic confetti, our hearts take a leap,
Sailing through stardust, in joy we will seep.
For longing is funny when laughter's our guide,
In constellations of whimsy, forever we glide.

When Fate Aligns

When planets align, it's a rather odd plot,
A twist on the tale that life forgot.
With fate tossing coins in a jester's bright hat,
We whirl in delight, what could be more fat?

We play peek-a-boo with the galaxies wide,
While fortune bemused takes us all on a ride.
Swapping our shoes with the universe's flair,
Turning mishaps to magic with cosmic repair.

A tumble through orbits, a barrel roll spin,
When mischief and fate decide to let us win.
With a comet's tail tickling our toes,
We giggle at gravity's unforeseen flows.

So here's to the chaos, the cosmic delight,
To fate's funny games that keep us in sight.
For when stars are mischievous, hearts intertwine,
In this wild ballet, we dance, feel divine.

Ephemeral Glows of Togetherness

We danced beneath the cosmic show,
With twinkling lights and laughter's flow.
Chasing dreams that flickered bright,
In a world that spun with sheer delight.

You tripped on stardust, giggles soared,
As I caught you, your laughter roared.
Among the sparks, we lost our way,
But love was bright, and here to stay.

Celestial Paradox of Touch

Your hand in mine, a twisted fate,
Like gravity and love, they wait.
A cosmic dance of wrong and right,
We laughed till dawn, hearts took flight.

With every poke, the universe grinned,
As we collided where stars had sinned.
You wore confusion like a crown,
Yet in this chaos, no one drowned.

When Time Stands Still in Nightfall

At midnight, we lost track of time,
With silly jokes and rhymes sublime.
The moon wobbled, sun forgot to rise,
As we played hide and seek with stars in the skies.

In this stillness, the cosmos giggled,
As we shared dreams and silly riddles.
Each moment stretched, a playful tease,
As laughter echoed through cosmic breeze.

Echoes of Love Across the Galaxy

Your voice reverberates through endless space,
In echoes of love, we found our place.
With comet tails and playful sighs,
Together we soared through alien skies.

We shot past planets, made quippy remarks,
As laughter lit up the darkest parks.
In a universe vast, with hearts on fire,
Our funny saga became our desire.

A Dance with the Cosmos

In a galaxy far, far away,
Two clumsy comets twirled and swayed.
They tripped on space dust, lost their way,
Laughed so hard, they could hardly stay.

The moon giggled at their silly flight,
While stars winked down with pure delight.
They spun in circles, what a sight!
In zero gravity, they took to night.

With dance moves that baffled every star,
One comet shouted, 'Hey, look at this spar!'
They pirouetted past Venus, oh my!
Even Mars tutted, 'They'll need a guide.'

But as they twirled in cosmic cheer,
The black hole teased, lurking near.
'Join us, silly nuts, have no fear!'
So they danced and danced, lost in the sphere.

The Milky Way of Dreams

In the Milky Way, where dreams collide,
A cow jumped over the moon, full of pride.
With stars complaining, 'She'll need a ride!'
While planets laughed, 'Come join us inside!'

A rocket ship was hosting a bash,
Inviting comets, all in a flash.
They brought their ice cream, made quite a stash,
But got distracted and ended up crashed.

The sun made cookies, oh, what a treat!
But those who tried burned their tongue in the heat.
They danced to gravity's funky beat,
While space squirrels scurried, quick on their feet.

And evergreen fairies sprinkling bliss,
Even asteroids threw a galactic kiss.
In this Milky Way dream, who could miss?
Laughter echoed throughout the abyss.

Fated Constellations

In skies of fate, two stars did meet,
One wore glasses, the other, a sheet.
They pondered, 'Is this love or a cosmic treat?'
Their shining halos sparkled, oh so sweet.

A wise old nebula came by to tease,
'Your pairing's absurd, laugh as you please!'
With goofy grins and wobbly knees,
They danced in the warmth of a whimsical breeze.

The Big Dipper spilled drinks, oh what a mess!
While Ursa Major wore a bright red dress.
They twirled and stumbled, 'What's this distress?'
But all were too busy to clean up the excess.

In the end, they felt quite grand,
Creating tales no one could understand.
While the universe giggled, hand in hand,
Fated constellations, a cosmic band.

Orbiting Your Heart

I'm orbiting around your heart, dear friend,
Like a tired planet searching for trend.
With gravity's pull, I start to blend,
But I accidentally hit that comet—oh, what a send!

You call out, 'Hey, watch where you're going!'
While I'm busy propelling and glowing.
With space debris flying and love overflowing,
It's hard to stop when the fun keeps growing.

But as I dance in my clumsy parade,
You snicker at my goofy charade.
While space aliens join in and invade,
We laugh till our stardust is homemade.

So let's whirl and twirl in this cosmic spree,
Your laughter's the best gravity for me.
In this endless waltz of infinity,
I'll orbit your heart for eternity!

Interstellar Affection

In the galaxy, I tripped on space,
Your love, my gravity, set the pace.
I orbit you like a satellite,
But stumble in love, what a sight!

At light speed, I'm losing my way,
A comet with toothpaste, hey ho, hooray!
Playful meteors throw a curve,
In this cosmic dance, we swerve!

Your laughter's like a supernova sight,
It lights up my world, oh what a delight!
Mars to my Venus, a comical twist,
In this universe, impossible to resist!

Alien jokes in our nightly chats,
Like UFOs wearing funny hats.
Our love's a moonwalk in clumsy shoes,
Stars wink at us; they can't help but muse!

Love's Celestial Map

I charted a course through the Milky Way,
But got lost somewhere in lunchtime play.
Your smile's a beacon, my course correct,
But with my direction? That's a wreck!

Galactic giggles echo in the night,
While nebulae swirl in comedic flight.
Asteroids dance with a silly grace,
As we navigate this outer space.

Your heart's a planet, filled with cheese,
In this quirky cosmos, I'm a breeze.
Orbiting closer makes us collide,
In this map of love, there's no guide!

We'll star hop through the laughter's scope,
Building a rocket ship of goofy hope.
Acidic stars and fiery trails,
In our universe, humor never fails!

Echoes of the Universe

Whispers between quasars, oh what fun,
In the void of space, we've just begun.
Our giggles resonate in the astral beam,
In a cosmic echo, we dare to dream.

Silly shadows dance on Jupiter's plains,
Like two clowns caught in celestial chains.
Wobbling through wormholes, we share a joke,
While Saturn's rings catch light like a cloak.

Through the laughter, I hear a shout,
In the vastness of space, you're what it's about.
Our love is an echo that won't fade away,
In this universe, come what may!

Galaxies chuckle at our clumsy flight,
As we dodge black holes with all our might.
In this playful void, we're never alone,
Each whisper is a love tone, all our own!

Constellation of Hearts

In the night sky, we create our map,
With heart-shaped stars and a goofy clap.
You wink like a comet that's lost its way,
While I laugh, dreaming of our cabaret.

A dipper of dreams, we mix and swirl,
In this cosmic dance, our hearts unfurl.
Your puns outshine the lunar glow,
Making me laugh as we drift and flow.

Meteor showers need our retakes,
We slip on stardust, causing a quake.
Constellations quirk in delightful cheer,
As our love spins in this cosmic sphere.

Together we shine, a luminous pair,
In this universe, no need to compare.
Our constellation tells a tale so bright,
Of two souls laughing into the night!

Luminous Threads of Destiny

In a café, fate spills its tea,
A meeting planned for two, oh glee!
But they tripped over their own small feet,
And ended up lost in a fine, tall seat.

Their eyes like comets, bright and wild,
One slight grin, the other beguiled.
They spoke of dreams, oh what a shock!
In cosmic chaos, time took stock.

A tangled dance of mismatched shoes,
A cosmic game of 'what's your muse?'
Their hearts entangled, in playful jest,
Two silly souls, just chasing the quest.

With laughter echoing through the stars,
They spun tales of love from alien bars.
Destiny chuckled, who would've guessed?
That fate would dress them in goofy zest.

Lunar Serenade for the Unseen

Under a moon that winked with flair,
Two shadows danced, without a care.
Each step a twist, each spin a spin,
Who knew love could start with a silly grin?

A serenade played on a rubber band,
A harp of laughter, so unplanned.
They sang of ducks, they sang of cheese,
In the audience, stars nodded, 'Please!'

With every note, the night grew bright,
Their chorus echoed 'til morning light.
A melody crafted from hiccup and cheer,
A symphony of giggles, oh so dear!

Yet dawn arrived with a yawn and stretch,
Both tripped on dreams, there's no way to sketch.
The lunar concert, a sight to behold,
In the dance of life, their story told.

Fractured Mirrors of Affection

Two odd reflections, grinning wide,
In mirrors cracked, they did not hide.
With each slight flaw, more laughter grew,
A portrait painted by playful few.

Each glance a riddle, a curious jest,
"Is that your nose or a funny quest?"
With winks and smiles, they made it work,
In fractured glass, love's playful smirk.

Like jigsaw pieces, a puzzle askew,
Finding the bits that fit like glue.
With hearts that giggled and eyes that shone,
In a messy dance, they'd laugh and moan.

So toast to the cracks that left them bright,
Their imperfections glimmered in soft twilight.
In the madness of mirth, they found a home,
Two silly souls forever to roam.

Gravity's Pull on Wandering Hearts

In the cosmos of chance, a fumble's tale,
Two souls collided, like ships on a sail.
With gravity's push and a humorous pull,
They laughed as love became quite the duel.

Each misstep taken, a giggle ensued,
The universe winks, 'A love that's renewed!'
They tripped through the stars, past planets and suns,
Dodging the glitches of fate's little puns.

In zero-gravity, they soared with delight,
Twisting and twirling in the cool cosmic night.
Hearts skipped like stones on a shimmering bay,
While gravity chuckled, "What a clumsy ballet!"

And so they floated like feathers in flight,
Two wayward hearts that just felt right.
In the chaos of love, they found their way,
With a laugh and a twirl, come what may.

Enigmas of Celestial Hearts

In a galaxy far, far away,
Two hearts collided, come what may.
A comet sneezed, oh what a sight,
Their love lit up the cosmic night.

She danced with moons, he tripped on stars,
Negotiated peace with little cars.
Asteroids laughed as they took the chance,
Gravity, meanwhile, just watched the dance.

They scribbled notes on Martian dust,
While Pluto rolled its eyes in disgust.
But love's a riddle, tangled and wild,
Even if at times it's simply mild.

So here's to the lovers, brave and bold,
Finding their way through space untold.
The universe laughs at their delight,
Two goofy hearts in endless flight.

Dawn's Embrace of a Fateful Love

In the dawn's light, two muffins baked,
One was sweet, the other flaked.
They met on a plate, oh what a tease,
One crumbed the other with joyful ease.

The toaster popped, with a cheerful sound,
As they laughed at love, all doughy and round.
Coffee brewed up a mischievous plot,
While syrup giggled, "Give it a shot!"

Sunny side up, they flipped their fate,
In the kitchen, they were quite the mate.
Cinnamon swirls and berry delight,
Two treats in a box, such a funny sight!

So here's to the breakfast of dreams and glee,
Love's a feast, come eat with me!
In every bite, a twist and a turn,
With every laugh, the flame will burn.

Celestial Whispers

The moon was eavesdropping, oh so sly,
While Venus winked to the wandering sky.
Stars played cards, betting their glow,
On who would win love's dizzying show.

"Is Mars a flirt?" asked the sparkling sun,
"Or just a planet that pretends it's fun?"
Jupiter chuckled with cosmic cheer,
"Love's orbit's wobbly; let's spin a sphere!"

Comets skated with tails ablaze,
While meteors danced in a dazzling craze.
Galaxies swirled in a spirited race,
As laughter echoed through infinite space.

So here's to the worlds in laughter so deep,
Wishing on wishes, take a cosmic leap.
For love, dear friends, is a playful quest,
With stellar humor, we are truly blessed.

Fractured Fate

In a bakery of dreams, fate made a mess,
Two pastries collided, causing distress.
"Are we croissants or just dough on a plate?"
A flaky question of delicious fate.

They rolled on shelves, both sweet and wrong,
Singing to the tune of a creaky song.
Buttercream swirled as they found their way,
In the oven's warmth, they began to play.

Flour flew high, and laughter erupted,
As rolling pins joined, completely corrupted.
But through the chaos, they found a spark,
In the heart of the dough, light lit up the dark.

So here's to the mishaps that love can unfold,
The broken biscuits that make life bold.
In the kitchen of fate, chaos and cheer,
Two fractured hearts make the best kind of beer!

Yearning Across Dimensions

In a parallel life, I'm a charming star,
But in this one, I can't get very far.
My love's in a galaxy, far out of reach,
Sending me signals, but can't hear a speech.

I write my sweet notes on a comet's tail,
Hoping it brings me a love without fail.
But gravity's cruel, pulling us apart,
Stuck in a loop, oh, this cosmic heart!

With a wink and a smile, I twist and I twirl,
In my dreams, she spins, oh that cosmic girl.
We dance on the wind, just a blink away,
But return to mundane, oh, what a cliché!

Yet here I remain, in this dimensional mess,
Longing for laughter, if only to impress.
So I'll wear my space pants with cosmic flair,
And dream of the day we'll meet in midair.

Heartbeats in the Void

My heart races fast in this vast emptiness,
Each beat echoes loud, a comical mess.
Thinking of Cupid with a quiver too small,
Shooting arrows that miss, oh, isn't love a ball?

In the expanse, my feelings float free,
Like a lost sock in the dryer, just me.
Falling for you through the vacuum of space,
What's it called? Right, eternal misplaced embrace!

The planets spin wildly, a dizzying dance,
While I stumble on comets, dreaming of chance.
Love letters written in stardust and gas,
But you don't even notice, says 'Where's my glass?'

Yet still I keep writing, though the ink's all gone,
For in this black hole, your smile is my song.
So if laughter's the key, let's shimmer and shine,
Two hearts laughing loud, what a cosmic design!

Dancing on Starlight

We twirl on starlight, it's quite a soft glow,
Swapping our secrets, in whispers we flow.
Each giggle ignites like a flare in the night,
While we swerve through the cosmos, oh what a sight!

Gravity's pull, it keeps tugging us close,
Yet the sun's blushing bright, it's playing the host.
With a flash and a wink, we leap through the air,
Floating like feathers, without any care.

My heart's a balloon, it's ready to pop,
As we dance through the dark, we'll never just stop.
You're a comet of laughter, my favorite delight,
In this cosmic cabaret, twirling through light!

So here's to the moments, so silly and bright,
Where giggles are planets, and joy takes its flight.
We'll shine like a nebula, bright in full view,
Two kids on the star's merry-go-round, just us two!

The Path of Constellations

Across great expanses, we follow the map,
A cosmic scavenger hunt, oh, what a trap!
Mapping the stars with crayons and dreams,
Drawing love's path in whimsical beams.

With every mishap, the universe chuckles,
Our hearts go zipping, just like little buckles.
As we stumble on stardust, a supernova's glow,
I ask if you're hungry, do black holes eat dough?

Let's chart out the skies, one star at a time,
Trading funny stories, all in silly rhyme.
As we giggle and fall, we're caught in delight,
A waltz through the cosmos, pure joy in the night.

So hand me that telescope, let's aim for the sun,
We're cosmic explorers, oh what goofy fun.
With each little laugh, we'll connect all the dots,
Drawing funny shapes in the celestial lots!

Bound by Constellations

Under twinkling lights we bicker,
Your snacks are all a bit too much,
You say I'm hopeless, a bad trickster,
Yet you keep craving my soft touch.

Our stars align in perfect chaos,
You with your quirks and me with mine,
We dance around like silly payoffs,
In this cosmic joke, oh so divine.

You laugh at my outlandish dreams,
I snicker at your wild hairdo,
In this galaxy, love's not as it seems,
Yet here we are, just me and you.

With laughter loud and hearts ablaze,
We spin and twirl through the night air,
In our own wacky, starry craze,
Each cosmic mishap, another dare.

Shadows of Love

In the moonlight, shadows play tricks,
I step on your toes, you laugh and jest,
Your dance is wild, a bag of mixed picks,
Yet in this mess, I feel so blessed.

We argue over whose turn it is,
To pick the movie for our night in,
Yet no one wins this quirky quiz,
The popcorn flies, we both break in.

With clips from space and silly tunes,
We groove like planets stuck in a spin,
Your goofball moves make me swoon,
In our cosmic flow, we always win.

Though shadows sway and light may fade,
Our laughter echoes, bright and clear,
In this dance, we aren't afraid,
Embraced by love, we persevere.

The Astral Embrace

Your gaze is sweet as candy stardust,
We float like comets, never in line,
You snort when you laugh; oh what a must,
This clumsy love, so unrefined.

We trip through constellations of wit,
My charm's a rocket — or is it a flop?
Yet still you giggle, not losing a bit,
In our lunacy, we'll never stop.

Chasing the moon with an old futon,
Our dreams get tangled like starry threads,
On this ride, no place to fawn,
Just laughter and love in our crazy beds.

Though galaxies swirl and time may race,
In your orbit, I find my place,
Two goofy souls with an awkward embrace,
Together we dance through cosmic grace.

Celestial Yearning

You say my jokes are out of this world,
Yet here I am with my goofy charm,
Across the skies our hearts unfurled,
In constellations, a cosmic alarm.

Your laughter's my favorite melody,
As we stumble through this endless play,
In the warmth of our quirky remedy,
Every day's a delightful fray.

An astral trip with no clear map,
Yet we weave through stars, hand in hand,
Entangled in love, perhaps just a clap,
In this universe, we've made our stand.

So here's to laughter, love's shining light,
In this odd dance of cosmic delight,
Through every starlit and clumsy night,
We embrace the joy, hold our quirks tight.

Heartstrings and Gravity

In the dance of love, we trip and fall,
Gravity laughs, it catches us all.
With tangled hearts and mismatched socks,
We navigate fate, like bewildered clocks.

Your gaze is like glue, I'm stuck to my seat,
We giggle about how we're naught but a treat.
Two clowns in a circus, our acts never blend,
Yet with every misstep, I love you, my friend.

In this carnival ride, we twist and we spin,
A smile on my face, the world wears a grin.
Though the universe frowns on our charming clums,
I wouldn't trade this joy for some cosmic sums.

Sometimes we soar, sometimes we crash,
Like a comet too close, a celestial bash.
Yet with every rebound, a new joke to tell,
In the chaos of love, somehow it's swell.

Lovers Among the Stars

Under the moon, we argue and bicker,
You say I'm too slow, I say you're too quicker.
While planets align to try and conjoin,
We're lost in a dance, both awkward and joint.

With laughter that echoes from here to the sun,
We stumble through stardust, forgetting the fun.
You reach for my heart, I dodge with a wink,
We're lovers among stars, or maybe just pink.

Through meteor showers, we dodge and we weave,
Like knights of the galaxy, but all we do is grieve.
For each time you jest, and I roll my poor eyes,
A galaxy chuckles, with twinkling surprise.

In this cosmic chaos, love's a grand jest,
With secrets unspoken, we giggle—the best!
So here's to our fate, as absurd as it seems,
We're lovers among stars—in the land of our dreams.

Cosmic Longing

From the moons of romance, to the suns of desire,
We chase after dreams, like a cat on a wire.
With each wish I make, we spin on a dime,
Caught between laughter and the whims of time.

Your texts are like comets, they flash and they flare,
While I'm on a quest, looking for love in thin air.
In perfect alignment, our jokes intertwine,
But sometimes I wonder, is the punchline divine?

From Pluto to Venus, we chase silly schemes,
Like kids on a playground, we're lost in our dreams.
Yet every mishap, every whimsical twist,
Brings me closer to you—oh, how could I resist?

So here's to the mess that this journey composes,
We bloom like wildflowers, midst moons and pink roses.
In this vast universe, where chaos does sing,
I find my heart longing for you, silly thing!

Unwritten Destinies

In a world of oddities, our fates intertwine,
With laughter as our compass, we'll be just fine.
You trip on my heart, and I stumble on yours,
Destinies penned in the ink of galore.

Through comets and quirks, our story unfolds,
With scribbles and doodles of adventures untold.
In the margins of chaos, we chase what we crave,
Laughing at fortunes, we're naught but a wave.

Every glance is a chapter, so wild, so grand,
Yet every arc bends on uncertainty's hand.
But here's the big twist, the joke of it all,
I'd choose this right mess, my love, over it all.

So let's write our script, with giggles and cheer,
In this cosmic theater, you're my star, my dear.
For love is a play, where we jest and we dream,
In the book of unwritten, you're my fave meme.

Glimmering Paths

Two lovers met by chance, oh what a sight,
With missteps and giggles, they danced through the night.

One tripped on a rock, fell right on his face,
She laughed till she cried, her charm filled the space.

Their paths intertwine like spaghetti on plates,
With forks of confusion, they navigate fates.
Through puddles of laughter, they jump and they splish,
Each moment a treasure, each flub a sweet dish.

They scribble their dreams on the back of a bus,
With crayons and hopes, they blend in the fuss.
A map made of giggles, they'll follow the signs,
To a world where all's silly, and love intertwines.

So here's to the mix-ups, the blunders, the fun,
In the chaos of love, they've already won.
With a wink and a nod, they take life in stride,
On glimmering paths, let their laughter be their guide.

Collision of Souls

It started with coffee and a sugar-filled scone,
She spilled all her latte; he laughed on his phone.
A clash of intentions, a comedic debacle,
Their eyes met like meteors, orbiting wobbles.

With hearts racing wildly, they stumbled through fate,
Accidentally in love, it felt rather great.
Their plans all awry, but who needs a plan?
When magic's in chaos, just stick to the jam.

He wore one mismatched sock, her hair's a wild feathery,

In the realm of the absurd, they thrived rather steadily.
A dance in the grocery, a twirl in the aisle,
Their quirky connection spread joy like a smile.

Two souls in collision, a laughter-filled flame,
In a universe playful, there's no need for shame.
So they brave the oddness, a beautifully spun,
In the comedy of life, they have already won.

Dreamers Under the Dome

Beneath the big top, the circus of dreams,
With clowns and balloons, and ice cream in streams.
Two dreamers unite, both wearing bright hats,
With juggling of hopes, and a troupe of fat cats.

They created a message on cotton candy skies,
With giggles and glitter, their hearts in disguise.
In a tent of delights, they spun tales of grand,
As feathers and laughter slipped right through their hands.

Each wish they had whispered was caught in the breeze,
Like dandelion wishes, they laughed as they seized.
With acrobats soaring and tightropes to tread,
Their love was the circus; the world was their bed.

So here in the dome, where dreams meet the day,
They twirl amidst laughter, bright colors at play.
Together as jesters, they dance and they roam,
Forever in joy, they make laughter their home.

Celestial Echoes

The stars above chuckle while planets collide,
As lovers exchange glances, it's hard to decide.
Should they leap to the moon, or just roll in the grass?
With wishes like rockets, they skip and they pass.

In a galaxy filled with the quirkiest sounds,
Their laughter rings out, like musical bounds.
With comets that wink and a sun that just beams,
They uncover the magic hidden in dreams.

They twirl through the cosmos with bubblegum grace,
Stumbling on stardust, each bump a new place.
In the realm of absurd, their hearts start to soar,
Echoes of silliness, who could ask for more?

So float through the heavens with joy as your steer,
In the crazy dance of love, there's nothing to fear.
For laughter is timeless, like space it expands,
In celestial echoes, together they stand.

www.ingramcontent.com/pod-product-compliance
Lightning Source LLC
Chambersburg PA
CBHW051645160426
43209CB00004B/802